P.S. I LOVE YOU FOUR
Welcome Baby

by Lynda Milligan & Nancy Smith

Book Production

Sharon Holmes – Editor, Technical Illustrator
Susan Johnson – Quilt Designer, Photo Stylist
Lexie Foster – Graphic Designer, Photography
Christine Scott – Editorial Assistant
Sandi Fruehling – Copy Reader
Brad Bartholomew – Photographer

Thanks

Sewers – Jane Dumler, Ann Petersen, Courtenay Hughes, Katie Wells
Quilters – Ann Petersen, Jane Dumler, Debra Geissler
Baby Furniture – Guys & Dolls, 13280 E Mississippi Ave, Aurora, CO 80012

Fabric Designers for Avlyn, Inc. • Publishers of Possibilities® Books
Home of Great American Quilt Factory, Inc.
www.greatamericanquilt.com • www.possibilitiesquilt.com
1.800.474.2665

P.S. I Love You Four – Welcome Baby
©2006 Lynda Milligan & Nancy Smith

ISBN: 1-880972-59-X

Sail Away

40 x 52″   6″ Block

See page 18 for a photo of a girl's quilt, Lily Rose, with applique in the border. For Lily Rose, cut 17 background squares 6½ x 6½″ to replace sailboat blocks. Background needed: 1¼ yards. Make 200% copies of lettering for name. Patterns on page 47.

See page 34 for examples of quilts made like Lily Rose but with applique on the plain squares. For these quilts, use cutting and yardage in paragraph above for applique backgrounds. Choose from appliques on pages 40-47, and photocopy to an appropriate size.

Yardage   Choose fabric with 42″ usable width.

Background	1⅓ yd
Contrasting fabric - 9-patches	¾ yd
White - sails	¼ yd
Green - boats	⅓ yd
Border 1	¼ yd
Border 2	¾ yd
Binding	½ yd
Backing	2¾ yd
Batting	44 x56″

Cutting   Cut strips from selvage to selvage.
*Cut in half diagonally.

Background	
9-patch blocks	7 strips 2½″ wide
sailboat blocks	85 squares 2½″
	*26 squares 2⅞″
Contrasting fabric - 9-patches	8 strips 2½″ wide
White	*26 squares 2⅞″
Green	3 strips 2½″ wide
Border 1	4 strips 1½″ wide
Border 2	5 strips 4½″ wide
Binding	5 strips 2½″ wide

Directions   Sew ¼″ seams unless otherwise noted.

1. NINE-PATCH BLOCKS: Make strip sets as shown. Press. Cut into 2½″ segments. Use segments to make 18 blocks. Press.

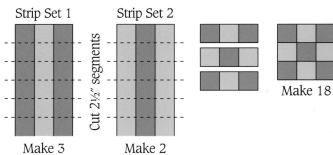

Strip Set 1   Strip Set 2

Cut 2½″ segments

Make 3   Make 2   Make 18

2. SAILBOAT BLOCKS: Cut green strips into 6½″ segments. Make 17 blocks following diagrams. Press.

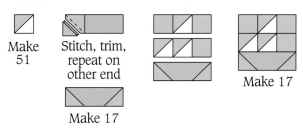

Make 51   Stitch, trim, repeat on other end   Make 17

Make 17

3. ASSEMBLE: Stitch blocks into horizontal rows as shown. Press. Stitch rows together. Press.

Continued on page 34

Sail Away

- Bib p 30
- Blanket 2 p 32
- Burp Cloth p 30
- Flange Pillow p 28
- Hat p 21
- Rectangular Pillow p 28

RESOURCES p 48

- ... & the Three Bears
- Quackers (duck)
- Ruffled Pillow
- Teddy Bear Magic

Jasmine

40 x 51″

See page 18 for a photo of another quilt, Razzle Dazzle, made with the Jasmine directions. Pattern and directions for scalloped border and binding are on page 34.

Yardage Choose fabric with 42″ usable width.

Center panel   1 yd if cutting on crosswise grain

1¼ yd if cutting on lengthwise grain

Border 1   ¼ yd
Border 2   ¾ yd
Binding   ½ yd - Jasmine
see page 34 for Razzle Dazzle

Backing   2¾ yd
Batting   44 x 57″

Cutting Cut strips from selvage to selvage.

Center panel   28½ x 39½″
Border 1   4 strips 1½″ wide
Border 2   4 strips 5¾″ wide
Binding   5 strips 2½″ wide - Jasmine
see page 34 for Razzle Dazzle

Directions Sew ¼″ seams unless otherwise noted.

1. BORDER 1: Cut 2 pieces to fit sides of center panel. Stitch to center panel. Press. Repeat at top and bottom.

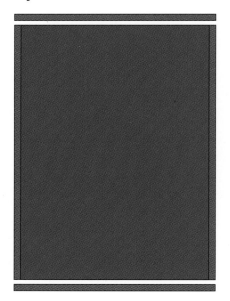

2. BORDER 2: Repeat Step 1.

3. LAYER & QUILT: Piece backing horizontally to same size as batting. Layer and quilt as desired. Trim backing and batting even with quilt top.

4. BIND: Stitch binding strips end to end. Press in half lengthwise, wrong sides together. Bind quilt using ⅜″ seam allowance.

Jasmine

- Bib p 30
- Crib Sheet p 33
- Diaper Bag p 22
- Flange Pillow p 28
- Kimono p 20
- Onesies p 24
- Pleated Crib Skirt p 33

RESOURCES P 48
- Baby Bumper Pads

Raspberry Splash

46 x 46″

See page 19 for a photo of another quilt, Choo Choo, made with the Raspberry Splash directions. Turn quilt so strips are horizontal and applique trains on wide strips. Patterns on page 41. Purchase applique fabric as needed, or use scraps.

Yardage
Choose fabric with 42″ usable width.

Center panel	⅔ yd for wide stripe
	⅜ yd each of 3 fabrics for narrow stripes
Border 1	¼ yd
Border 2	¾ yd
Binding	½ yd
Backing	3 yd
Batting	50 x 50″

Cutting
Cut strips from selvage to selvage.

Center panel	3 pieces 6½ x 36½″ from ⅔-yd piece
	2-4 pieces 2½ x 36½″ from each of the others
Border 1	4 strips 1½″ wide
Border 2	5 strips 4½″ wide
Binding	5 strips 2½″ wide

Directions
Sew ¼″ seams unless otherwise noted.

1. CENTER PANEL: Arrange three 6½″ strips and nine 2½″ strips in order shown. Stitch strips together. Press.

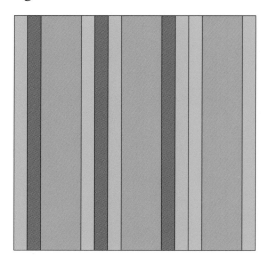

2. BORDER 1: Cut 2 pieces to fit sides of center panel. Stitch to center panel. Repeat at top and bottom.

3. BORDER 2: Stitch strips end to end with straight, not diagonal, seams. Press. Cut 2 pieces to fit sides of center panel. Stitch to center panel. Repeat at top and bottom.

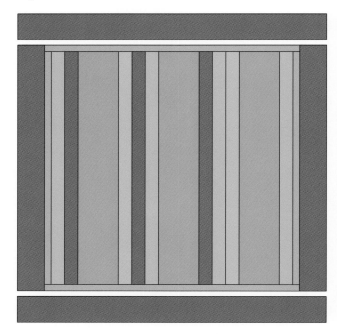

4. LAYER & QUILT: Piece backing to same size as batting. Layer and quilt as desired. Trim backing and batting even with quilt top.

5. BIND: Stitch binding strips end to end. Press in half lengthwise, wrong sides together. Bind quilt using ⅜″ seam allowance.

42 x 50″   8″ Block

See page 19 for a photo of another quilt, Penguin Parade, made with the County Fair directions. (Additional yardage: red accent fabric, ¼ yard. Applique fabrics: ¼ yard black; ⅛ yard each of white and yellow OR use scraps.) For blocks, make 4 half-square triangle units with red fabric and block background fabric. Make 4 blocks with a red unit in one corner. For Border 2, make 6 half-square triangle units with red fabric and Border 2 background fabric (white) and scatter them in Border 2. Applique pattern for Border 3 is on page 44.

Yardage Choose fabric with 42″ usable width.

Blocks	large pinwheel	½ yd
	small pinwheel in center	⅓ yd
	small pinwheel in corner	¼ yd
	background	¾ yd
Border 1		⅜ yd
Border 2		⅜ yd each of 2 fabrics
Border 3		⅞ yd
Binding		½ yd
Backing		2⅞ yd
Batting		46 x 54″

Cutting Cut strips from selvage to selvage.
*Cut in half diagonally.

Blocks	large pinwheel	48 pieces 2½ x 4½″
	small pinwheel in center	48 squares 2½″
	small pinwheel in corner	*24 squares 2⅞″
	background	*24 squares 2⅞″
		96 squares 2½″
Border 1	4 strips 2½″ wide	
Border 2	*34 squares 2⅞″ of each fabric	
Border 3	5 strips 5½″ wide	
Binding	5 strips 2½″ wide	

Directions Sew ¼″ seams unless otherwise noted.

1. BLOCKS: Make 12 blocks. Press.

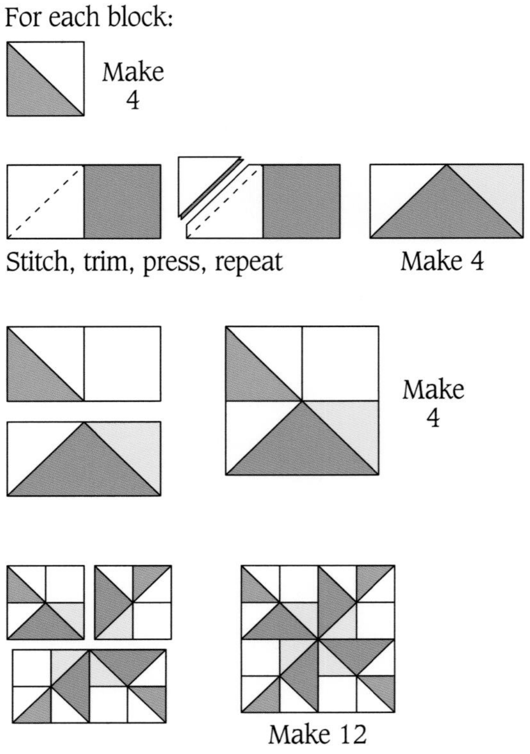

For each block:

 Make 4

Stitch, trim, press, repeat   Make 4

  Make 4

Make 12

2. ASSEMBLE: Stitch blocks into horizontal rows. Press. Stitch rows together. Press.

Continued on page 35

County Fair

- Bib p 30
- Blanket 1 p 32
- Burp Cloth p 30
- Changing Pad p 23
  (in diaper bag)
- Crib Sheet p 33
- Diaper Bag p 22
- Hat p 21
- Onesies p 24

RESOURCES p 48

- ... & the Three Bears
- Baby Bumper Pads
- Gathered Dust Ruffle
- Nurture Nest
- Quackers

Lil' Duds

45 x 30″

Yardage
Choose fabric with 42″ usable width.

Applique	¼ yd each of 3 fabrics - overalls
	⅙ yd each of 3 fabrics - shirts
	⅛ yd each of 6 fabrics - hats, etc.
Applique bkgrounds	⅓ yd each - blue, yellow, green
Sashing	⅓ yd each - black & white
Star blocks	¼ yd - red
	⅙ yd - green
	⅓ yd each - blue & yellow
Border	½ yd - blue
Border corners	⅙ yd each - red & yellow
Binding	½ yd
Backing	1½ yd
Batting	49 x 34″

Cutting
Cut strips from selvage to selvage.
*Cut in half diagonally.

Applique	patterns on pages 42-43
Applique bkgrounds	3 pieces 9½ x 16½″
Sashing	6 pieces 2½ x 5½″ - white
	4 pieces 2½ x 12½″ - white
	6 pieces 2½ x 5½″ - black
	2 pieces 2½ x 12½″ - black
Star blocks	*10 squares 2⅞″ - red
	32 squares 1½″ - red
	*10 squares 2⅞″ - yellow
	8 squares 2½″ - green
	paper-pieced side units - blue & yellow - pattern on page 43 - make 32 copies
Border	2 pieces 3½ x 24½″
	2 pieces 3½ x 39½″
Border corners	4 squares 3½″
Binding	4-5 strips 2½″ wide

Directions
Sew ¼″ seams unless otherwise noted.

1. APPLIQUE: Applique 4 corner squares with stars centered. Applique 3 Lil' Duds blocks with clothes centered side to side and ⅞″ from top and bottom edges.

 Make 4

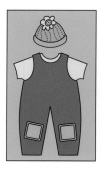  

2. STAR BLOCKS: Make 8 partial blocks following diagrams. Press. Remove foundation paper. Reserve extra units for sashing.

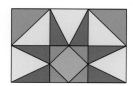

Paper Piece 32   Make 20   Stitch   Trim

Press   Make 8

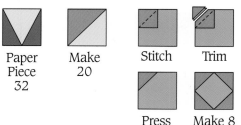

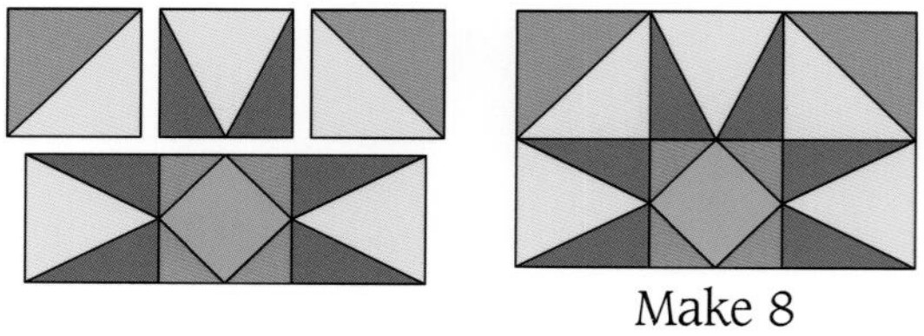

Make 8

3. SASHING: Make units as shown using light and dark sashing pieces and reserved star units. Press. Stitch sashing units, partial star blocks, and Lil' Duds blocks into horizontal rows as shown in diagram on page 37. Press. Stitch rows together. Press.

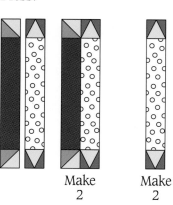

Make 2   Make 2   Make 6

10

Continued on page 37

Lil' Duds page 10
Ollie's Overalls page 17

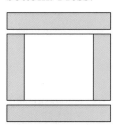

44 x 44″   6″ Block

Choose 21 photos that can be cropped square.

Yardage Choose fabric with 42″ usable width.

Photo fabric	EQ Printables Premium Cotton Lawn Inkjet Fabric Sheets - 1 package of 6 fabric sheets - see Resources, page 48
Borders 1, 3, 5	¾ yd
Border 2, Border 6 star blocks	½ yd each of 2 fabrics
Borders 4, 6	⅓ yd each of 10 or more fabrics
Border 7	⅜ yd
Binding	½ yd
Backing	3 yd
Batting	48 x 48″

Cutting Cut strips from selvage to selvage.
*Cut in half diagonally.

Borders 1, 3, 5	3 strips 2½″ wide - Borders 1, 3 4 strips 3½″ wide - Border 5
Border 2	*12 squares 2⅞″ of each fabric 4 squares 2½″ of outside fabric
Border 6 stars	*16 squares 2⅜″ of each fabric 16 squares 2″ background 4 squares 3½″ star fabric
Border 4	total of 22 pieces 2½ x 4½″
Border 6	1-2 strips 1¾″ wide of each fabric - photo blocks
Border 7	5 strips 1¾″ wide
Binding	5 strips 2½″ wide

Directions Sew ¼″ seams unless otherwise noted.

1. PHOTOS: Following manufacturer's directions, transfer photos to fabric sheets using your inkjet printer. Size center photo to 8½″ square, knowing you will lose ¼″ of image to seam allowance all around square. Print on one fabric sheet. Use remaining 5 sheets for 20 small photos, sizing them to 4″, knowing you will lose ¼″ to seam allowance all around square. Remove paper backing.

   Cut center photo transfer 8½″ square. Cut Border 6 photo transfers 4″ square.

2. BORDER 1: Cut 2 pieces to fit sides of center photo. Stitch to sides. Press. Repeat at top and bottom. Press.

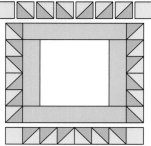

3. BORDER 2: Make 24 half-square triangle units. Press. For each side, stitch 6 units together as shown. Press. Stitch one border to each side of center block. Press. Stitch background squares to each end of remaining borders. Press. Stitch to top and bottom. Press.

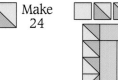

Make 24

4. BORDER 3: Cut 2 pieces to fit sides of quilt. Stitch to sides. Press. Repeat at top and bottom.

5. BORDER 4: Stitch 5 pieces together for each side border. Press. Stitch to sides of quilt. Press. Repeat for top and bottom borders using 6 pieces.

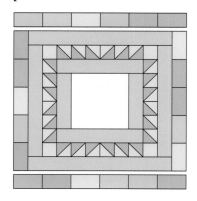

6. BORDER 5: Cut 2 pieces to fit sides of quilt. Stitch to sides. Press. Repeat at top and bottom.

Continued on page 36

Picture Perfect

RESOURCES P 48

53 x 53″   9″ Center Blocks

Yardage
Choose fabric with 42″ usable width.

Center blocks, Borders 1, 5, & applique

	⅓ yd each of 4 fabrics - orange, gold, yellow (Piece F of center blocks & others)
	¼ yd each of 12 or more fabrics - orange, gold, yellow, pink, purple, turquoise, teal, green, blue
Border 2	½ yd yellow
	⅙ yd gold/pink/purple
Border 3	¼ yd orange
Border 4	¼ yd lavender
Border 5	⅜ yd purple/turquoise
Border 6	½ yd each yellow & lavender
	¼ yd each orange & turquoise
Border 7	⅓ yd purple
Border 8	⅝ yd purple/turquoise
Binding	⅝ yd
Backing	3½ yd
Batting	57 x 57″

Cutting
Cut strips from selvage to selvage.

Center blocks	make 4 copies of pattern piece D, page 38 for paper piecing - cut 4 sets of fabric pieces from patterns A-F (except D), pages 38-39
Border 1	8 pieces 2½ x 6½″ - orange, gold
	16 squares 2½″ - assorted fabrics
Border 2	4 strips 3½″ wide - yellow
	4 squares 3½″ - gold/pink/purple
Border 3	4 strips 1½″ wide
Border 4	4 strips 1″ wide
Border 5	4 strips 2½″ wide - purple/turquoise
	12 squares 2½″ - assorted fabrics
Border 6	8 pieces 6½ x 9″ - yellow
	8 squares 6½″ - lavender
	4 squares 6½″ - orange
	4 squares 6½″ - turquoise
Border 7	5 strips 1½″ wide
Border 8	6 strips 2½″ wide
Applique	make 200% copies of patterns on page 40 before tracing to fusible web
Binding	6 strips 2½″ wide

Directions
Sew ¼″ seams unless otherwise noted.

1. CENTER BLOCKS: Paper piece 4 unit D using 2 fabrics for each unit. Stitch pieces A-F together, matching center marks and outside edges of pieces. Make 4. Stitch 4 blocks into center unit. Press.

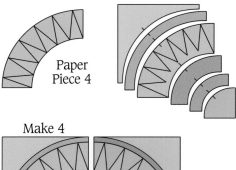

Paper Piece 4

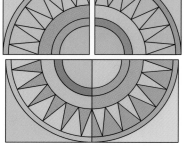

Make 4

2. BORDER 1: For sides, stitch 2 rectangles and 3 squares together as shown. Press. Stitch to sides of center unit. Repeat for top and bottom borders using 2 rectangles and 5 squares.

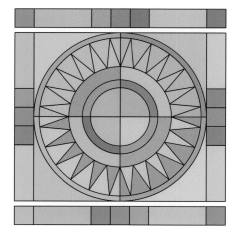

Continued on page 37

14

Good Morning Sunshine

- Blanket 1 p 32
- Flange Pillow p 28
- Kimono p 20
- Onesies p 24
- Rectangular Pillow p 28

RESOURCES p 48
- Teddy Bear Magic

Pocket Playtime

46x46″ 10″ blocks, 8″ pockets

Photo on page 7

See notes on handling Oh! So Soft on page 32

Yardage

Choose fabric with 42″ usable width.

Center panel	⅔ yd cotton or Oh! So Soft (poly velour)
Blocks, pocket centers, pocket linings	⅝ yd each of 6 fabrics
Pocket frames	¼ yd each of 6 fabrics
Border	⅝ yd
Binding	½ yd
Backing	3 yd
Batting	50x50″

Cutting

Cut strips from selvage to selvage. Preshrink all cotton fabrics - Oh! So Soft does not shrink.

Center panel	20½x20½″
Blocks	10½″ squares - 2 from each fabric
Pocket centers	5½″ squares - 2 from each fabric
Pocket linings	8½″ squares - 2 from each fabric
Pocket frames	4 strips 1¼″ wide from each fabric
Border	5 strips 3½″ wide
Binding	5 strips 2½″ wide

Directions

Sew ¼″ seams unless otherwise noted.

1. ASSEMBLE: Stitch block squares and center panel into rows. Stitch rows together. Press.

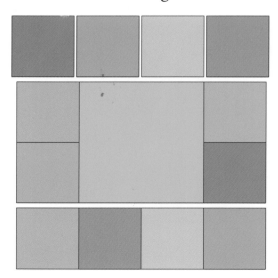

2. POCKETS: Pick 2 frame strips for each pocket. Cut 2 pieces 5½″ long and 2 pieces 7″ long from strip chosen for inside frame. Stitch short pieces to sides of center square. Press. Stitch long pieces to top and bottom. Press. Repeat with strip chosen for outside frame, cutting side pieces 7″ long and top/bottom pieces 8½″ long. Make 12.

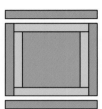

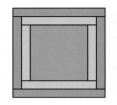

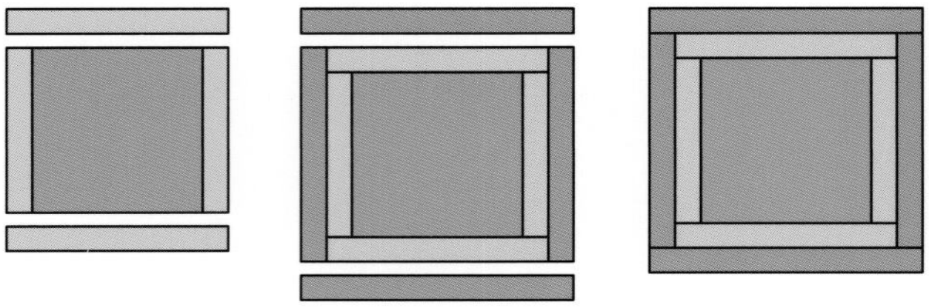

Place pocket and pocket lining square right sides together. Stitch around square, leaving an opening on one side for turning. Clip corners, turn right side out, and press. Stitch opening closed. Repeat with remaining 11 pockets.

3. BORDER: Stitch strips end to end with straight, not diagonal, seams. Press. Cut 2 pieces to fit sides of quilt. Stitch to quilt. Repeat at top and bottom.
4. LAYER & QUILT: Piece backing to same size as batting. Layer backing, batting, and quilt top. Quilt in the ditch between 10″ blocks. If center panel is Oh! So Soft, it can be quilted less densely than rest of quilt. Finish quilting as desired, including inside 10″ blocks. Trim backing and batting even with quilt top. See diagram on page 35.
5. POCKETS: Pin pockets to blocks, centered. Pocket openings can face center panel of quilt or they can face in different directions. Use side where opening was stitched closed as bottom edge of pocket. Topstitch 3 edges of each pocket, backstitching to secure ends. For extra strength, quilt around each pocket, approximately ⅛-¼″ away. See diagram on page 35.

Continued on page 35

Ollie's Overalls

42 x 48″

Photo on page 11

Yardage
Choose fabric with 42″ usable width.

Applique	⅙ yd each of 4 fabrics - pocket, hat, star
	¼ yd - shirt
	½ yd - overalls
Corner blocks	¼ yd - background
	⅛ yd - centers
	⅙ yd - star points
Center panel	⅞ yd
Border 1	¼ yd
Border 2	¼ yd each - black & white
Border 3	⅞ yd
Binding	½ yd
Backing	2⅞ yd
Batting	46 x 52″

Cutting
Cut strips from selvage to selvage.

Applique	make 200% copies of patterns on pages 42-43 before tracing to fusible web
Corner blocks	16 squares 2½″ - corners
	4 squares 2½″ - centers
	paper-piece side units - pattern on page 43 - make 16 copies
Center panel	26½ x 32½″
Border 1	4 strips 1½″ wide
Border 2	30 pieces 1½ x 2½″ - white
	34 pieces 1½ x 2½″ - black
Border 3	4 strips 6½″ wide
Binding	5 strips 2¼″ wide

Directions
Sew ¼″ seams unless otherwise noted.

1. APPLIQUE: Applique overalls and hat to center panel, centered from side to side and 1¼″ from top and bottom edges.

2. CORNER BLOCKS: Make 4 blocks following diagrams. Press. Remove paper.

For each block:

Paper
Piece 4

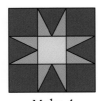

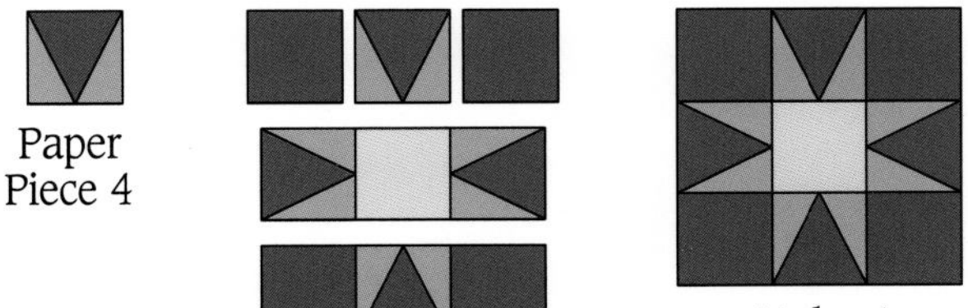

Make 4

3. BORDER 1: Cut 2 pieces to fit sides of center panel. Stitch to center panel. Press. Repeat at top and bottom.

4. BORDER 2: For each side, stitch 17 black and white pieces together, starting and ending with black. Repeat for top and bottom with 15 pieces each. Press. Stitch side borders to quilt. Press. Stitch top and bottom borders to quilt. Press.

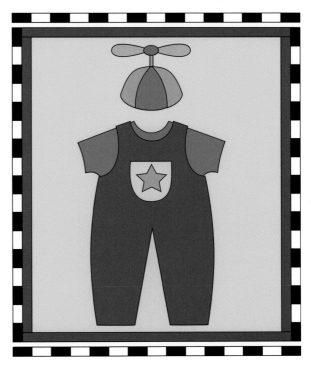

5. BORDER 3: For sides, cut strips to same length as quilt. For top and bottom, cut strips to same width as quilt. Stitch star blocks to each end of top and bottom borders. Stitch side borders to quilt. Press. Stitch top and bottom borders to quilt. Press. Diagram on page 36.

Continued on page 36

17

Lily Rose page 2

Razzle Dazzle page 4

Penguin Parade page 8
Onesies p 24
Penguin p 24

Choo Choo page 6

19

• • • Kimono • • •

6-12 month - Photos on pages 5 & 15
See section at end of directions for yardage and cutting adjustments for 12-18 month size. Optional applique patterns on pages 40-47. Purchase applique fabric as needed, or use scraps.

Yardage Choose fabric with 42″ usable width.

Kimono	⅔ yd
Lining	⅔ yd
Binding, pocket, ties	½ yd

Cutting Cut strips from selvage to selvage.

See paragraph and diagrams at end of directions for cutting size 12-18 month.

Back	11″ wide x 12¼″ long - 1 each of kimono fabric & lining - 12¼″ side on lengthwise grain
Front	9½″ wide x 12¼″ long - 2 each of kimono fabric & lining - 12¼″ side on lengthwise grain
Sleeve	10½″ wide x 7½″ long - 2 each of kimono fabric & lining - 7½″ side on lengthwise grain
Pocket	1 piece 6″ wide x 9″ long
Ties	2 pieces 2½ x 20″
Binding	3 strips 2″ wide

Directions Sew ¼″ seams unless otherwise noted.

1. FURTHER CUTTING: Cut neckline, front diagonal, and sleeve sides of kimono and lining pieces. See paragraph and diagrams at end of directions for cutting size 12-18 month.

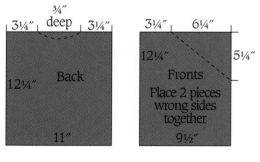

2. SHOULDER SEAMS: Stitch shoulder seams of kimono pieces. Press seam allowances open. Repeat with lining pieces.

3. SLEEVE SEAMS: Find center of long side of kimono sleeve. Place right sides together on front/back of kimono, center of sleeve on shoulder seam. Stitch. Press seam allowance toward sleeve. Repeat for other kimono sleeve. Repeat with lining pieces.

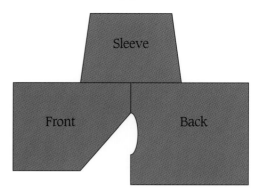

4. POCKET: Fold pocket in half right sides together, to 6x4½″. Draw a 2½″ circle at each bottom corner as shown. Cut curves at corners. Stitch, leaving an opening at bottom edge for turning. Turn right side out. Stitch opening closed. Press. Applique pocket if desired. Pin pocket to left front of kimono, 1¼″ from bottom edge and 1½″ from front edge. Topstitch in place.

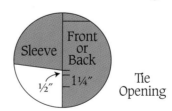

5. SIDE SEAMS: Mark for tie opening on left side of both kimono and lining.

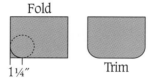

With right sides together, pin side seams of kimono from bottom edge of sleeve to bottom edge of front/back. Stitch, pivoting at underarm, leaving marked spot for tie open. Clip into seam allowance at underarm. Press seam allowances open. Repeat with lining.

6. TIE: Fold each tie piece in half lengthwise, right side inside. Stitch one end and the long side. Trim corners, turn right side out, and press. Baste unfinished end of tie to front, right sides together, raw edges even, ½″ down from point as shown. Repeat with remaining tie on other front.

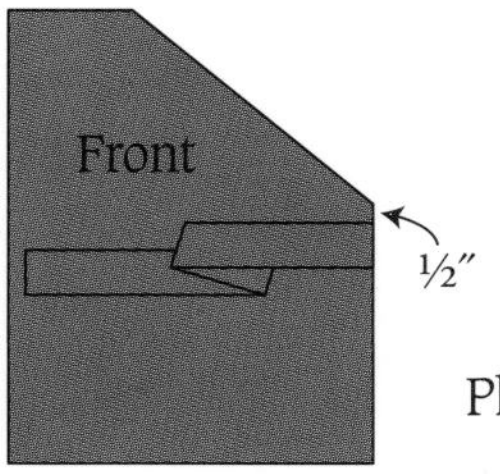
Front
½″

Tie Placement

7. PIN LINING TO KIMONO: Place kimono and lining wrong sides together. Pin at side seams, shoulder seams, and along front edge. Be careful not to stretch the bias neck edge.
8. BIND: Stitch binding strips end to end. Press in half lengthwise, wrong sides together. Starting at center back on right side of kimono, with raw edges even, stitch binding to kimono bottom, front, and neck edges. Miter corners. Turn folded edge of binding to lining side, overlapping stitching line by approximately ⅛″. Pin binding in place from right side. Stitch in the ditch on right side. Bind sleeves at wrist.
9. FINISH TIES: To secure each tie, fold it over binding and topstitch in place. Finish tie opening in side seam by machine or hand stitching edges together.
10. Place kimono on baby, insert right tie end through side opening, and tie at center back.

12-18 MONTH SIZE:
Increase yardage of kimono and lining to ¾ yd
Cut backs 12½″ wide x 14¼″ long
Cut fronts 10½″ wide x 14¼″ long
Cut sleeves 11½″ wide x 9″ long
Cut pocket 6¼″ wide x 9″ long

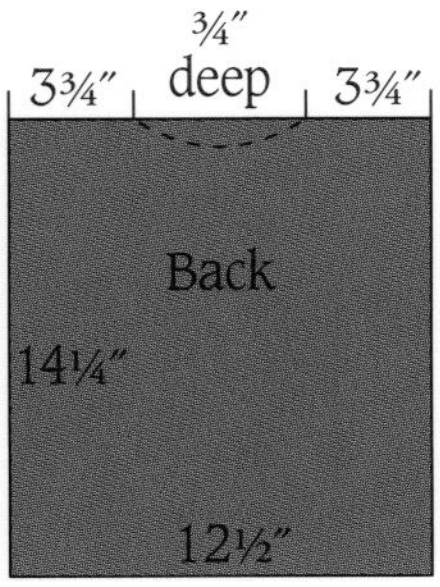
¾″
3¾″
deep
3¾″
Back
14¼″
12½″

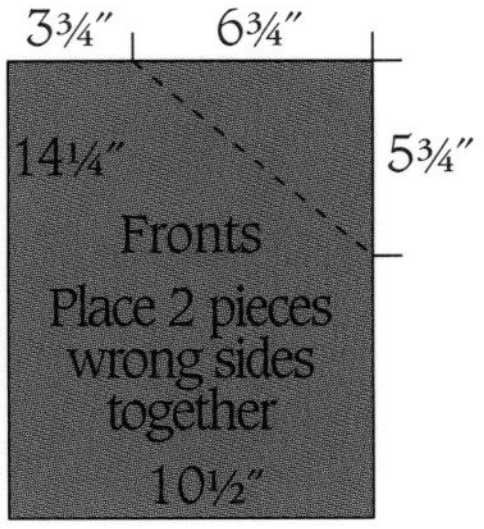
3¾″
6¾″
14¼″
5¾″
Fronts
Place 2 pieces wrong sides together
10½″

• • • Hat • • •

S 19″, M 20″, L 21″
Photos on pages 3, 9, & 11

Supplies
Choose fabric with 42″ usable width.

Hat	⅜ yd each of 2 fabrics - outside & lining
Opt. 2nd crown fabric	⅙ yd
Hat brim	¼ yd
Opt. propeller	⅛ yd fabric
	⅛ yd Peltex® Ultrafirm Stabilizer - double-sided fusible
	buttons & beads - see Step 6

Cutting
Hat
- 8 crown pieces for outside all of 1 fabric or 4 each of 2 fabrics - patterns on page 40
- 8 crown pieces for lining
- 2 tie pieces 2x14″
- 2 brim pieces patterns on page 40 - place 2 pieces of fabric right sides together & cut out together

Directions
Sew ¼″ seams unless otherwise noted.

1. Alternating fabrics if using 2, stitch outside crown pieces together in sets of 2. Stitch sets of 2 into sets of 4. Stitch sets of 4 into circular crown. Repeat for lining, leaving a 3″ opening in last seam for turning.
2. Fold each tie piece in half lengthwise, right side inside. Stitch one end and long side. Trim corners, turn right side out, and press. Pin or baste one tie to each side of crown lining, raw edges even, right sides together.
3. Stitch short edges of each brim piece together, making a circle. Place brim circles right sides together, and stitch shaped edge. Clip, turn right side out, and press.
4. Stitch a single line of gathering $\frac{3}{16}$″ from raw edges of brim. Fold in half, then quarters, and mark with pins. Pin to outside crown of hat, right sides together, matching pins in brim to every other crown seam. Gather brim to fit crown, and distribute gathers evenly. Pin crown lining, right sides together, to brim and outside crown. Stitch seam. Turn right side out through opening in lining. Stitch opening closed. Press seam between crown and brim.
5. Tack outside crown and lining together at top or securely stitch button, or other decorative element such as silk flower, to top.

Continued on page 30

• • • Diaper Bag • • •

14″ wide x 14″ high x 6″ deep
Photos on pages 5 & 9. Optional applique patterns on pages 40-47. Purchase applique fabric as needed, or use scraps.

Supplies Choose fabric with 42″ usable width.

Main fabric	⅞ yd
Lining, inside pockets	1 yd
Pockets, outside	⅝ yd
Trim	⅓ yd
Handles	⅝ yd
Batting - thin cotton	19x42″ - bag
	2 pieces 8x10″ - pockets
	2 pieces 2⅜x53″ - handles

Clear elastic - ⅜″ wide
Velcro® - 2″ piece
Optional - 6x14″ plastic needlepoint canvas - rigid bottom
¼ yd lining fabric for covering canvas

Cutting Cut strips from selvage to selvage.

Main fabric	19x42″
Lining	18x41″
	2 pieces 12x14″ - inside pockets
	2 pieces 5x12″ - inside pockets
Pockets, outside	2 pieces 10x16″
	2 pieces 7x16″ - main fabric or outside pocket fabric
Trim	1 piece 5x41″ - top edge
	1 strip 2½″ wide - lg outside pockets
Handles	3 strips 5″ wide

Directions Sew ¼″ seams unless otherwise noted.

1. QUILT: Layer batting and main fabric. Quilt parallel lines. Trim rectangle to 18x41″.

2. TOP TRIM: Draw a line on right side of bag 4½″ from top edge. Place trim on bag, right sides together, along line. Stitch. Fold trim to right side and press. Quilt trim to bag with horizontal lines.

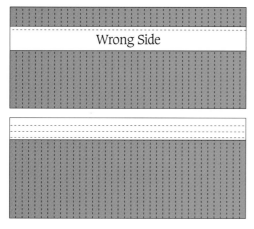

3. LARGE OUTSIDE POCKETS: Make 2. Press pocket pieces in half, wrong sides together, to 8x10″. Fold is bottom of pocket. Slide batting between layers. Quilt pockets diagonally in both directions or as desired. Trim edges even. Press pocket trim in half lengthwise, wrong sides together. Bind top edges of pockets. Applique pockets, if desired.

4. SMALL OUTSIDE POCKETS: Make 2. Press pocket pieces in half, right sides together, to 7x8″. Fold is top of pocket. Stitch around pocket, leaving an opening on bottom edge for turning. Clip corners. Turn right side out. Stitch opening closed. Press. Draw a line 1½″ from top edge on inside of pocket. Cut elastic 4½″ long. Backstitch end of elastic to one side of pocket on drawn line. Using a zigzag stitch and stretching as you go, stitch elastic along line, ending with a 1″ tail. Backstitch. Trim end of elastic. Pin a ½″ pleat at each side of bottom edge, ½″ in from each side.

5. HANDLES: Stitch handle strips end to end and cut 2 pieces 54″ long. For each handle, center batting on wrong side of fabric. Press short fabric ends over batting. Press long edges of fabric over batting to meet in center. Fold strip in half lengthwise and press well (double thickness of batting, 1¼″ wide). Pin. Topstitch close to all edges and again ¼″ away.

6. ATTACH HANDLES & OUTSIDE POCKETS: Pin large outside pockets to bag. Stitch close to lower edges and again ¼″ away. Pin handles to bag, covering raw side edges of pockets. Topstitch along previous stitching lines on handles, stopping at lower edge of trim along top of bag. Pin small pocket to bag, centered between large pockets. Stitch close to side and bottom edges. Stitch side seam of bag. Center remaining small pocket over side seam and stitch in place.

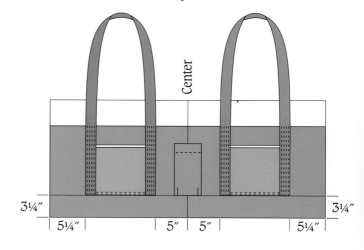

7. BOX BOTTOM: Stitch bottom seam of bag. Fold bottom corners of bag with side of bag matched to bottom seam. Mark box-bottom seams 3″ from point as shown. Stitch on marked lines. Turn right side out.

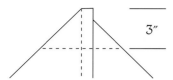

8. LINING & INSIDE POCKETS: Make 2 of each size pocket. Press small pocket pieces in half, right sides together, to 5x6″. Fold is top of pocket. Repeat with large pocket pieces (12x7″). Stitch around each pocket, leaving openings on bottom edges for turning. Clip corners. Turn right side out. Press. Pin two large and one small pocket(s) to lining as shown. Stitch close to side and bottom edges. Stitch another vertical line on one or both large pockets, if desired, to divide into smaller pockets. Stitch side seam of lining. Center remaining pocket on seam and stitch to lining. Press. Sew bottom seam of lining, leaving approximately 6″ open for turning. Make box corners in lining. See Step 7 above.

Place lining and bag right sides together. Stitch top edge. Turn right side out through opening in lining. Tack lining and bag together at box bottom triangles. Stitch opening closed. Topstitch close to top edge of bag. If desired, continue topstitching lines on handles to top edge of bag, or topstitch each handle parallel to top edge of bag leaving part of handle free in which to tuck burp cloth or other small item. Stitch 2″ pieces of Velcro® to top of bag on inside, centered between handles.

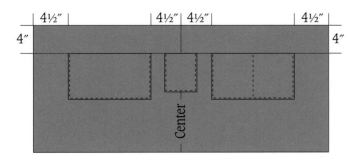

9. OPTIONAL BOTTOM INSERT: Cut 1 piece of fabric 6¾x29″. Fold in half, right sides together, to 6¾x14½″. Stitch long sides. Turn right side out. Insert needlepoint canvas. Hand stitch opening closed.

• • • Changing Pad • • •

20x30″ - Photo on page 9

Supplies Choose fabric with 42″ usable width.

Flannel - front	¾ yd
Cotton fabric backing, binding, casings	1 yd
Batting	22x32″
Elastic - ½″ wide	½ yd

Cutting Cut strips from selvage to selvage.

Flannel	22x32″
Cotton	22x32″
	2 pieces 2x15″ - elastic casings
	3 strips 2½″ wide - binding

Directions

1. Layer flannel (wrong side up), batting, and fabric (right side up). Pin baste. Machine quilt a diagonal 3″ grid. Trim to 20x30″.

2. Stitch long side of elastic casing piece. Turn right side out. Insert 9″ piece of elastic and stitch elastic securely to casing at each end. Make 2. Make a loop with each elastic/casing. Pin raw edges to one short edge of changing pad, on cotton fabric side, 4″ from corners.

3. Stitch binding strips end to end. Press in half lengthwise, wrong sides together. Bind raw edge of changing pad using a ⅜″ seam allowance, catching elastic/casings in stitching.

4. Starting at end without elastic/casings, roll changing pad with flannel inside. Pull elastic/casing over each end of roll.

23

• • • Penguin • • •

6x7″ - Photo on page 19
See notes on handling Oh! So Soft on page 32

Supplies

Front	¼ yd black cotton or Oh! So Soft
	¼ yd white - tummy & foundation
	⅛ yd yellow
Backing	¼ yd black print
Fusible web	¼ yd
Stuffing	small amount
Optional bow	¼ yd ¼″-wide ribbon

Directions

1. Make a 200% copy of penguin pattern on page 44. Trace body (including head, back, and tail, but not tummy or top wing) on fusible web. Trace top wing, tummy, and beak separately (do not trace bow, feet, or other wing tip). Following manufacturer's directions, fuse body and top wing to black fabric, tummy to white fabric, and beak to yellow fabric. Cut out. Use press cloth when fusing Oh! So Soft.

2. Cut 8x10″ piece of white fabric for foundation. Cut 8x10″ piece of backing.

3. Fuse penguin to foundation. Applique with a machine blanket or satin stitch.

4. Place penguin applique right sides together with backing. Stitch around penguin very close to applique stitching, leaving an opening for turning.

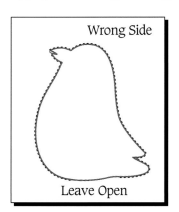

Wrong Side

Leave Open

5. Trim backing and foundation, leaving a ¼″ seam allowance. Clip. Turn right side out. Stuff firmly. Stitch opening closed.

6. For optional bow, tie ribbon into a bow and tack securely to penguin at neck.

• • • Onesies • • •

Embellished with Applique & Hot Fix Crystals
Photos on pages 5, 7, 9, 11, 13, 15, 18, & 19

Supplies

Purchased onesie
Scraps of applique fabrics or hot fix crystals

Directions

APPLIQUE: Choose an applique from pages 40-47. Resize on a photocopier if necessary. Applique on purchased onesie, using stabilizer on back.

HOT FIX CRYSTALS: For safety, prewash onesies to remove finish and sizing that can interfere with bond between garment and crystals.

Choose one of the designs on page 25 or create your own arrangement.

Spray a light mist of temporary spray adhesive (such as Sulky KK 2000™) on the area of the onesie where the design will go. Set hot fix crystals in place with tweezers. Set dry iron to the proper temperature for the onesie. Use wool setting for cottons. Place iron on crystals for 25-45 seconds. Do not move iron. Turn item over and press again from the back. Cool for about 3 minutes. For safety, it is essential to test for a permanent bond between crystals and garment. If not, reposition iron and heat again. Onesie can be gently machine washed and dried.

There are several helpful tools and materials on the market for applying hot fix crystals. They include heat application tools such as the BeJeweler™, and clear mylar adhesive sheets for positioning crystals. Follow manufacturers' directions for the use of these items.

Dyeing Onesies
For some fun custom colors, follow manufacturer's directions on Dylon® Permanent Fabric Dye package.

star Oh Baby!

CUTE A ☆

STUFF IS BORN

• • • Sling • • •

Short, Medium, & Long Sizes
Optional applique patterns on pages 40-47.
Purchase applique fabric as needed, or use scraps.

Supplies Choose quilting-weight cotton fabric.

Short   2⅛ yd each of 2 fabrics - 1 outside & 1 lining
Medium   2⅜ yd each of 2 fabrics - 1 outside & 1 lining
Long   2⅝ yd each of 2 fabrics - 1 outside & 1 lining
Rings   two 3″-diameter 4-gauge (¼″ thick)
                metal - hardware stores
Velcro®   2″ piece

Cutting

Small   27½ x 72″
Medium   27½ x 81″
Large   27½ x 90″
Pocket   1 square 10½″ from each fabric
Facing   1 piece 3 x 5¼″

Directions Sew ¼″ seams unless otherwise noted.

1. Place sling pieces right sides together. Trim one end on dotted lines as shown.

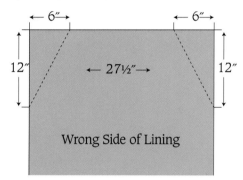

2. Leaving untrimmed end open, stitch around sling. Clip corners, turn right side out, and press. Topstitch close to seamed edges.

3. Place pocket pieces right sides together. Stitch around pocket, leaving an opening for turning. Clip, turn right side out, and press. Applique pocket, if desired. Center pocket on lining side of trimmed end of sling, 2-3″ from lower edge. Topstitch in place close to edge and again ¼″ away. Stitch Velcro® pieces to pocket and sling at center top of pocket.

4. Pleat open end to 4½″ wide, outside fabric showing on both sides of pleated bundle, 6 thicknesses. Press pleats to 12″ from raw ends. Stitch across pleats close to raw ends. Tuck 4″ of pleated end through both rings so that raw edges are on outside (right side) of sling. For shoulder cap, pull one pleat (2 layers) away from others on side without raw edges. Pin remaining pleats in place. Stitch securely through all layers approximately ½″ from raw ends, leaving the shoulder cap unstitched.

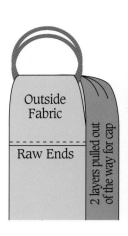

5. Fold facing in half, to 1½ x 5¼″. Stitch around raw edges, leaving an opening on long side for turning. Clip, turn right side out, and press. Pin in place over raw edges of sling and topstitch close to edge and again ¼″ away.

Laura and Adin Serota

Test sling for safety before using with baby.

26

• • • Soft Photo Book • • •

10 x 10" - Additonal photo on page 13
Choose 12 photos, 1 per page, including covers.
Optional applique patterns on pages 40-47. Purchase
applique fabric as needed, or use scraps.

Supplies Choose fabric with 42" usable width.

Photo fabric	EQ Printables Premium Cotton Lawn Inkjet Fabric Sheets - 1-2 packages of 6 fabric sheets - see Resources, page 48
String quilting	¼ yd each of 10-14 fabrics
Paper - foundations	4 squares 10½" - cover
	8 squares 10¼" - inside pages
Muslin - stabilizer	¾ yd
Batting - ultrathin (Thermore®)	1 piece 10½ x 20½" - cover

Cutting Cut strips from selvage to selvage.

String quilting	30-40 strips of varying widths: from 1" to 3½"
Muslin	1 piece 10½ x 20½" - cover
	2 pieces 10¼ x 20" - inside pages

Directions Sew ¼" seams unless otherwise noted.

1. Following manufacturer's directions, transfer photos to fabric sheets using your inkjet printer. Size photos as desired, but not larger than 6 x 6". Cut out transfers, knowing you will lose ¼" on each side to seam allowance. Remove paper backing.

2. String quilt around transfers on paper foundations. Use 10½" foundation squares for covers, page 1, and page 10. Use 10¼" foundation squares for remaining pages. Use wider strips at outside edge. Do not remove paper yet.

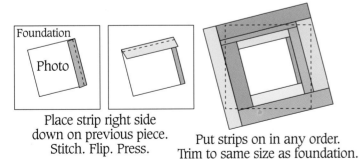

Place strip right side down on previous piece. Stitch. Flip. Press.

Put strips on in any order. Trim to same size as foundation.

3. With right sides together, stitch completed pages together in pairs, leaving an opening for turning on pages 1/10, 3/8, and 7/4 (see diagram next column). Tear off paper. Add applique, if desired.

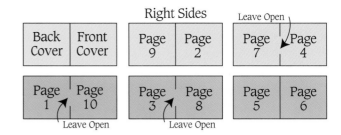

4. Baste batting and muslin to wrong side of cover ³⁄₁₆" from edge. Baste muslin to wrong sides of pages 9/2 and 5/6.

5. Place cover right sides together with pages 1/10. Stitch around entire outside edge. Clip corners, grade seam allowances, turn right side out, and press. Turn in seam allowance at opening and hand stitch closed. Repeat with pages 9/2 and 3/8. Repeat with pages 7/4 and 5/6.

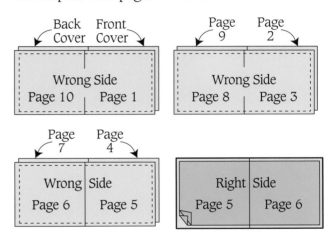

6. Place book cover open on flat surface with pages 1/10 facing up. Centering smaller pages on larger ones, place page 2 face down on page 1, page 4 face down on page 3. Check sequence of pages. Pages 5/6 will be facing up. Turn book over and machine stitch in seam at center, hand wheeling thickest part at each end if necessary. Backstitch at each end to secure pages.

• • • Rectangular Pillow • • •

12x16″ - Photos on pages 3 & 15

Supplies Choose fabric with 42″ usable width.

Front	6-10 fabrics ⅛ yd each
Envelope back	½ yd
Binding	½ yd
Batting - thin	15x19″
Pillow form	12x16″

Cutting Cut strips from selvage to selvage.

Front	10 strips of varying widths: from 1¼″ to 3″
Envelope back	2 pieces 14x21″
Binding	2 strips 6½″ wide

Directions Sew ¼″ seams unless otherwise noted.

1. Use strips to string quilt on batting at an angle, 30° or so. Press. Trim to 14x18″.

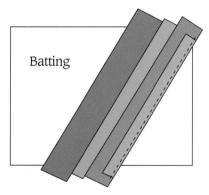

2. With wrong sides together, press envelope backing pieces in half, to 14x10½″. Place backing pieces on wrong side of pillow top, raw edges matching, folded edges overlapping at center of pillow. Stitch around outside edge with ⅞″ seam allowance.

3. Stitch binding strips together end to end. Press in half lengthwise, wrong sides together. Bind pillow using 1″ seam allowance, mitering each corner.

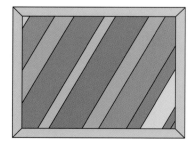

4. Insert pillow form.

• • • Flange Pillow • • •

12x12″ - Photos on pages 3, 5, 11, & 15
Optional applique patterns on pages 40-47.
Purchase applique fabric as needed, or use scraps.

Supplies Choose fabric with 42″ usable width.

Envelope back & flange front	⅞ yd
Center square	⅜ yd
Border 1	⅛ yd
Border 2	⅛ yd
Batting - thin	16½x16½″
Pillow form	12″

Cutting Cut strips from selvage to selvage.

Envelope back & flange front	2 pieces 22x16½″ 2 strips 2½″ wide
Center square	1 square 9½″
Border 1	1 strip 1″ wide
Border 2	2 strips 1½″ wide

Directions Sew ¼″ seams unless otherwise noted.

1. Cut 2 Border 1 pieces 9½″ long. Stitch to sides of center square. Repeat at top and bottom with pieces cut 10½″ long. Press. Repeat for Border 2 with 2 pieces cut 10½″ long and 2 pieces cut 12½″ long. Repeat for flange with 2 pieces cut 12½″ long and 2 pieces cut 16½″ long. Applique center square, if desired. Baste batting to wrong side of pillow front ⅛″ from edge. Quilt as desired.

2. Fold envelope back pieces in half, wrong sides together, to 11x16½″. Place backing pieces on right side of pillow front, raw edges matching, folded edges overlapping at center of pillow. Stitch around entire outside edge. Clip corners, turn right side out, and press.

3. Topstitch through all layers between flange and Border 2 as shown.

4. Insert pillow form.

• • • Photo Pillow • • •

14 x 14″ - Photo on page 13
Choose 1 photo that can be cropped square.

Supplies   Choose fabric with 42″ usable width.

Photo fabric	EQ Printables Premium Cotton Lawn Inkjet Fabric Sheets - 1 package of 6 fabric sheets - see Resources, page 48
Star block	⅛ yd each of 2 fabrics - star points & background
Border 1	⅛ yd
Border 2	¼ yd
Envelope back	½ yd
Pillow form	14″

Cutting   Cut strips from selvage to selvage.
Cut in half diagonally.

Star block	4 squares 2¾″ - background
	*4 squares 3⅛″ - background
	*4 squares 3⅛″ - star points
Border 1	1 strip 1″ wide
Border 2	2 strips 2½″ wide
Envelope back	2 pieces 14½ x20″

Directions   Sew ¼″ seams unless otherwise noted.

1. Following manufacturer's directions, transfer photo to fabric sheet using an inkjet printer. Size to 5″ square, knowing you will lose ¼″ of image to seam allowance all around square. Cut photo transfer 5″ square. Remove paper backing.

2. Make star block. Press.

Make 8
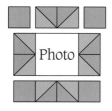
Make 4
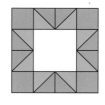

3. Cut 2 Border 1 pieces 9½″ long. Stitch to sides of star block. Repeat at top and bottom with pieces cut 10½″ long. Press. Repeat for Border 2 with 2 pieces cut 10½″ long and 2 pieces cut 14½″ long.

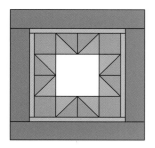

4. Fold envelope back pieces in half, wrong sides together, to 14½ x10″. Place backing pieces on right side of pillow front, raw edges matching, folded edges overlapping at center of pillow. Stitch around entire outside edge. Clip corners, turn right side out, and press.

5. Insert pillow form.

• • • Nurture Nest • • •

20 x 24″
Additional photo on page 9

Use this unique pillow for nursing and for supporting and exercising baby.

Purchase Nurture Nest form by Fairfield. See Resources, page 48. Pattern and full directions are included in package.

Make Nurture Nest cover with cotton fabric on both sides, or make one side flannel or Oh! So Soft. Add loops of various ribbons in seam, if desired. An 18″ or 20″ zipper is recommended.

Adin Serota

Blanket 1 - p 32
Teddy Bear Magic - p 48

29

• • • Bib • • •

S & L sizes. Photos on pages 3, 5, 7, 9, 11, & 18.
Optional applique patterns on pages 40-47. Purchase
applique fabric as needed, or use scraps.

Yardage

Bib fabric & flannel   ⅜ yd each
Binding   ⅓ yd

Cutting

Bib fabric	2 pieces 8x8″ - small
	2 pieces 10x10″ - large
optional pocket	2 pieces 10x3″ - large
Flannel	1 piece 8x8″ - small
	1 piece 10x10″ - large
Binding	**bias** strips 2¼″ wide to measure the following when sewn end to end: small - 70″ large - 85″

Directions   Sew ¼″ seams unless otherwise noted.

1. If desired, stitch optional applique to bib.

2. Pin bib pieces wrong sides together with flannel
   in between. Pin pocket pieces wrong sides
   together. For small bib, make a circle pattern 3½″
   in diameter (4″ for large). Using pattern, trim all
   corners of bib and 2 corners of pocket. Using
   same pattern, mark and cut neck opening on top
   edge of bib (half circle).

3. Stitch bias strips end to end, right sides together.
   Press seams open. Press in half lengthwise, wrong
   sides together.

4. Pin raw edges of binding to straight edge of
   pocket. Stitch. Fold binding to back, enclosing
   raw edge and stitch in ditch from right side. Baste
   pocket to bottom edge of bib. Bind all but neck
   edge of bib in same way as pocket.

Large   Small

5. Cut 40″ length of binding for neck edge/tie.
   Mark center of binding and center of neck edge.
   Matching centers, pin binding to neck edge. Stitch
   neck edge. Fold binding to back, enclosing raw
   edge at neck. Pin. Fold ties, enclosing raw edges.
   Pin. Stitch from one end of tie, along neck edge,
   to other end of tie. Trim tie ends to desired length
   and tie a knot in each end.

• • • Burp Cloth • • •

Photos on pages 3, 9, 11, & 13

Supplies

Purchased diaper with padded center panel
¼ yd cotton fabric

Directions

Cut a piece of fabric 1″ larger than padded center
panel of diaper. Press ½″ to wrong side on all edges.
Pin to diaper and topstitch in place.

• • • Hat • • •

Continued from page 21

6. Optional Propeller: Following manufacturer's
   directions, fuse fabric, wrong side down, to both
   sides of 2x6″ piece of Peltex®. Cut out propeller
   using pattern on page 40. Satin stitch edge, going
   around twice for full coverage. Stitch propeller
   securely to top of hat using large flat button (¾-1″
   diameter) on inside of hat for stability, and stack-
   ing buttons and beads to about ½″ on outside of
   hat to lift propeller off surface. Stack small button
   and bead on top of propeller also. To tack brim of
   propeller beanie to crown, fold brim up and stitch
   securely to crown with buttons on every other
   point (6 buttons needed).

• • • Play Ball • • •

7″ diameter

Photos on pages 7 & 13

Supplies

Fabric scraps at least 6″ square - 12
Ribbons - ¼ yd each of 10 different colors & designs
Stuffing

Cutting

12 pentagons - pattern includes seam allowance
29 pieces of ribbon 3″ long

Directions   Use ¼″ seam allowance.

1. Fold each piece of ribbon in half, and as you stitch each seam, place one somewhere in the seam, raw edges matching. Stitch 6 pentagons together in numerical sequence following diagram, beginning and ending stitching ¼″ from each edge. Make 2.

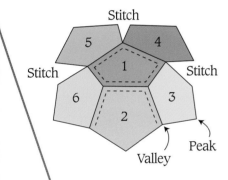

2. Matching peaks to valleys, stitch 2 halves together, leaving one edge open for stuffing. Stitch a ribbon into each seam with the exception of the one left open for stuffing.

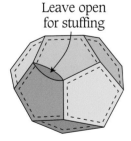

3. Turn; stuff firmly. Fold raw edges in and whipstitch opening closed.

• • • Play Blanket • • •

19″ square

Photos on pages 7 & 18
See notes on handling Oh! So Soft on page 32

Supplies

Oh! So Soft (poly velour)   ⅔ yd each of 2 fabrics
Ribbon   ¼ yd each of 10 different
                                                 colors & designs

Cutting

Oh! So Soft   2 squares 20″
Ribbon   28 pieces 3″ long

Directions

1. Trim corners of Oh! So Soft squares to a rounded shape about the diameter of a drinking glass.

2. Make a loop with each piece of ribbon. Pin or baste raw edges of ribbon loops to right side of one square of Oh! So Soft. Place 7 loops on each side, evenly spaced.

3. Matching lengthwise grain, pin or baste second square of Oh! So Soft right sides together to square with ribbons. Stitch around edge using ½″ seam allowance, leaving an opening for turning.

4. Turn right side out. Slip stitch opening closed. Topstitch ⅜″ from edge.

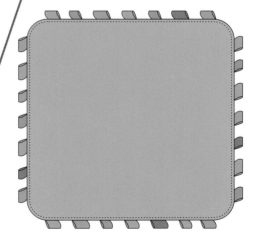

• • • Blanket 1 • • •
Oh! So Soft & Flannel with Self Binding
40x40″

Photos on pages 9, 13 & 15

Notes on Handling Oh! So Soft (poly velour): Easy care 100% polyester won't shrink. Handles like a knit. Stable lengthwise, stretchy on crossgrain. Nap is directional. Use even-feed foot when sewing. Press on wrong side with nap side against a bath towel, or use pressing cloth. Use synthetic setting and light pressure when ironing.

Yardage Choose fabric with 42″ usable width.
1¼ yd flannel - preshrink before cutting
1⅜ yd Oh! So Soft

Cutting
Cut a 40″ square of flannel - remove selvage edges & mark lengthwise grain
Cut 44″ square of Oh! So Soft - mark lengthwise grain

Directions
1. Center flannel wrong sides together on Oh! So Soft, matching grain lines. Pin in place. Machine stitch 2 or 3 equally spaced lines in one direction, or in both directions to make large squares, just enough stitching to hold layers together.

2. Starting in center on one side, fold edge of Oh! So Soft to edge of flannel, then fold over another inch, creating a 1″-wide double-thick finish. Pin to flannel on all four sides, leaving corners unpinned.

3. Trim corner diagonally as shown, 2″ from corner of flannel. Fold Oh! So Soft over flannel at corner. Fold edges in to create mitered corner.

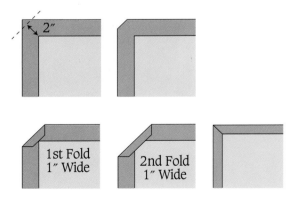

4. Using a zigzag stitch and an even-feed foot, stitch along edge. Topstitch mitered corners in place.

• • • Blanket 2 • • •
Flannel with Wide Contrasting Binding
40x40″

Photos on pages 3, 11 & 13

Yardage Choose fabric with 42″ usable width.
1¼ yd each of 2 flannels
⅞ yd cotton fabric for binding

Directions
1. Cut 1 square of each flannel, 40x40″. Pin squares wrong sides together. Machine stitch 2 or 3 equally spaced lines in one direction, or in both directions to make large squares, just enough stitching to hold layers together.

2. Cut 5 strips of binding 5″ wide (cut from selvage to selvage). Stitch binding strips together end to end. Press seam allowances open. Press ½″ to wrong side on each long edge. Press binding in half lengthwise, wrong sides together, so one side is slightly wider than the other.

Begin attaching binding at the middle of a side, rather than at a corner. Leave an 8″ tail of binding. Place binding around edge of blanket, wider edge on bottom, narrower edge on top, edge of blanket at fold line of binding. Attach binding with a medium-wide open zigzag. Stop stitching at edge of blanket and backstitch. Cut threads. Press miter. Resume zigzag stitching at inside corner and continue to edge of blanket as before. Repeat until 12″ from beginning. Join ends of binding so it will fit remaining section. Zigzag binding to remaining section of blanket.

Hand stitch miters in place on both sides of blanket.

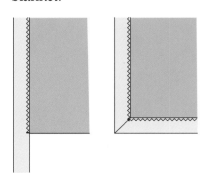

Optional Applique
Personalize your baby blanket with your choice of applique. See pages 40-47.

• • • Crib Sheet • • •

To fit a standard crib—mattress 27x52″

Photos on pages 5, 9, 11 & 13

Supplies

Fabric - **must have 43″ usable width**	2 yd
¼″ elastic	1 yd
½″ single-fold bias tape - optional	4½ yd

Directions   Use ¼″ seam allowance.

1. Cut a 43x68″ rectangle of fabric. Mark and cut an 8″ square from each corner.

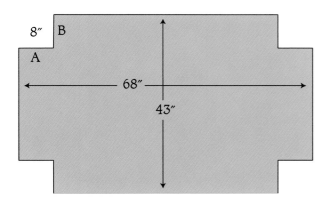

2. With right sides together, pin edge "A" to edge "B" at each corner. Stitch.

3. To bind edges using bias tape: Fold bias tape in half lengthwise and press. Slip folded edge over raw edge of sheet and pin. Machine stitch bias tape using a straight stitch or a small zigzag. Stitched hem: Press a ¼″ double hem to wrong side. Stitch next to fold.

4. Pin the center of a 9″ piece of elastic to the wrong side of each sheet corner with the edge of the elastic about ⅛″ from bias tape or hemmed edge. Machine stitch from this center point along elastic with a zigzag stitch, stretching elastic as tight as possible. Start from center and stitch to end of elastic. Repeat for other end of elastic. Repeat for other three corners.

• • • Pleated Crib Skirt • • •

To fit a standard crib—mattress 27x52″

Photo on page 5

Yardage   Choose fabric with 42″ usable width.

Fabric	5¾ yd

Cutting   Remove selvages before cutting.

1 piece 27x52″ - center panel
6 pieces 24½″ by width of fabric

Directions   Use ¼″ seam allowance.

1. For side panel of crib skirt, stitch two 24½″ pieces right sides together to make one piece 24½″ by about 84″. Repeat for other side panel. Press seam allowances open. Trim each side panel to 76½″ long.

2. Fold side panel in half lengthwise, right side inside. Stitch ends. Turn right side out and press. Repeat with other side panel. Mark each side panel into quarters lengthwise, creating four 19″ sections. Pin or baste 2″ pleats on each side of each mark.

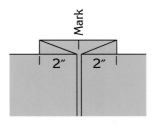

Trim remaining two 24½″ pieces to 35½″ long for end panels of crib skirt. Fold in half lengthwise, right side inside. Stitch ends, turn right side out, and press. Mark each end panel in half lengthwise, creating two 17½″ sections. Pin or baste 2″ pleats on each side of each mark.

3. Stitch side panels to center panel, right sides together, raw edges matching. Repeat with end panels. Press seam allowances toward center panel. Topstitch seam allowances to center panel ⅛″ from edge.

Sail Away

Continued from page 2

4. BORDER 1: Stitch strips end to end using straight, not diagonal, seams. Press. Cut 2 pieces to fit sides of quilt. Stitch to quilt. Repeat at top and bottom.

5. BORDER 2: Repeat Step 4.

6. LAYER & QUILT: Piece backing horizontally to same size as batting. Layer and quilt as desired. Trim backing and batting even with quilt top.

7. BIND: Stitch binding strips end to end. Press in half lengthwise, wrong sides together. Bind quilt using ⅜″ seam allowance.

Examples of other quilts using Sail Away directions. See second paragraph on page 2.

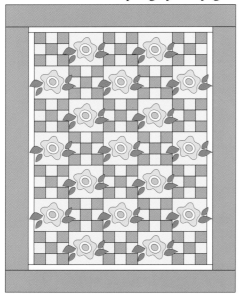

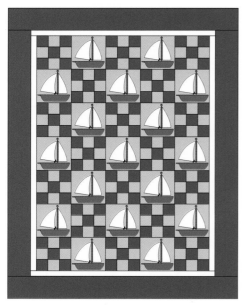

Razzle Dazzle

Continued from page 4 – photo on page 18

Follow yardage, cutting, and directions for Jasmine, page 4, except for quilting and binding. Follow directions below for marking scalloped border, quilting, and bias binding.

SCALLOPED BORDER & BIAS BINDING

Mark scallops before layering and quilting. Make plastic or paper template from pattern below. Find center point of each side of quilt top. To mark scallops, start at center of one side. Place straight side of template along outer edge of border with center of curved edge at center of border. Mark number of scallops shown in diagram. Repeat on other sides. Template will overlap approximately ¾″ at each corner. Do not cut scallops until quilting is completed. Layer and quilt. Machine stitch around quilt just inside marking for scallops, then trim batting, backing, and quilt top along scallop marking. Cut **bias** strips 1½″ wide to measure approximately 250″ after stitched end to end. Apply binding in single layer, without folding it in half as for double binding. Pivot at inside corners to form miters.

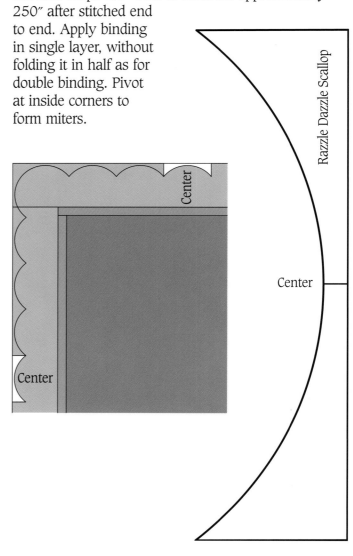

Razzle Dazzle Scallop

Center

Center

Center

County Fair

Continued from page 8

3. BORDER 1: Cut 2 pieces to fit sides of quilt center. Stitch to quilt. Press. Repeat at top and bottom.

4. BORDER 2: Make 68 half-square triangle units. Stitch units into borders as shown. Press. Stitch side borders to quilt, oriented as shown. Press. Repeat with top and bottom borders.

Sides - 18 Units - Make 2

Top/Bottom- 16 Units - Make 2

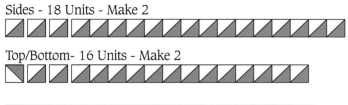

5. BORDER 3: Stitch strips together end to end with straight, not diagonal, seams. Press. Cut 2 pieces to fit sides of quilt. Stitch to quilt. Press. Repeat at top and bottom.

6. LAYER & QUILT: Piece backing horizontally to same size as batting. Layer and quilt as desired. Trim backing and batting even with quilt top.

7. BIND: Stitch binding strips end to end. Press in half lengthwise, wrong sides together. Bind quilt using ⅜″ seam allowance.

Pocket Playtime

Continued from page 16

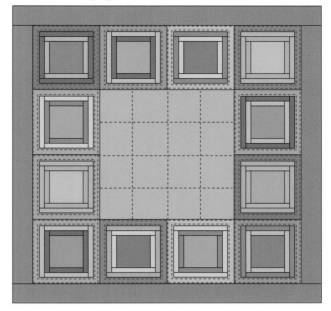

6. BIND: Stitch binding strips end to end. Press in half lengthwise, wrong sides together. Bind quilt using ⅜″ seam allowance.

7. Place toys in pockets as shown on page 7.

Good Morning Sunshine

Continued from page 37

7. BORDERS 7 & 8: Stitch strips end to end. Press. Cut 2 pieces to fit sides of quilt. Stitch to sides. Press. Repeat at top and bottom. Applique suns to top and bottom borders, centering them on remaining turquoise squares with rays overlapping blocks and borders to each side.

8. LAYER & QUILT: Piece backing to same size as batting. Layer and quilt as desired. Trim backing and batting even with quilt top.

9. BIND: Stitch binding strips end to end. Press in half lengthwise, wrong sides together. Bind quilt using ⅜″ seam allowance.

Picture Perfect
Continued from page 12

7. BORDER 6: For star blocks, make 32 half-square triangle units. Press. Stitch into pairs as shown. Press. Make 4 blocks. Press.

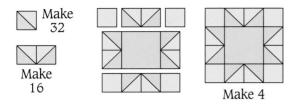

Make 32

Make 16

Make 4

Photo Blocks: Cut 2 pieces to fit sides of photo. Stitch to sides. Press. Repeat at top and bottom. Make 20.

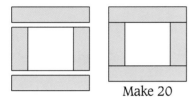

Make 20

For each side, stitch 4 photo blocks and 1 star block together in order shown. Press. Stitch to quilt, oriented as shown. Repeat for top and bottom with 6 photo blocks and 1 star block.

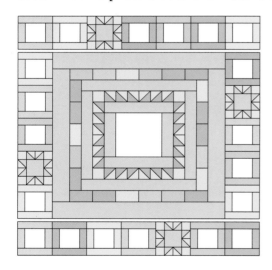

8. BORDER 7: Stitch strips end to end with straight, not diagonal, seams. Press. Cut 2 pieces to fit sides of quilt. Stitch to quilt. Repeat at top and bottom.

9. LAYER & QUILT: Piece backing to same size as batting. Layer and quilt as desired. Trim backing and batting even with quilt top.

10. BIND: Stitch binding strips end to end. Press in half lengthwise, wrong sides together. Bind quilt using ⅜″ seam allowance.

Ollie's Overalls
Continued from page 17

6. LAYER & QUILT: Piece backing horizontally to same size as batting. Layer and quilt as desired. Trim backing and batting even with quilt top.

7. BIND: Stitch binding strips end to end. Press in half lengthwise, wrong sides together. Bind quilt using ¼″ seam allowance.

• • • Pieced Bumpers • • •

Photo on page 11
To fit a standard crib—mattress 27x52″
Purchase Baby Bumper Pads by Fairfield. See Resources, page 48.

SUBSTITUTE YARDAGE: 6 black & white fabrics, ½ yd each, for fronts - 4 bright accent fabrics, ⅙ yd each - 1 backing fabric, 1¾ yd - four ⅝″-wide ribbons, 4 yd each, for ties - 7 yd jumbo rickrack

ADDITIONAL DIRECTIONS: Cut 2 squares 11¾″ of each black and white fabric for fronts. Cut 6 pieces of brights 3x11¾″. Cut 6 pieces of brights 2¾x11¾″. Cut 6 backings 27x11¾″. Use diagram to piece 6 bumper fronts with ⅜″ seam allowance, inserting rickrack in seams. Use basic bumper directions in package to complete bumpers, substituting 20″ pieces of ribbon for fabric ties.

Cut size 5x11¾″

Cut size 2¾x11¾″

Good Morning Sunshine

Continued from page 14

3. BORDER 2: Cut 4 yellow strips 22½" long. Stitch one yellow piece to each side of quilt. Press. Stitch corner squares to each end of remaining pieces. Press. Stitch to top and bottom of quilt. Press.

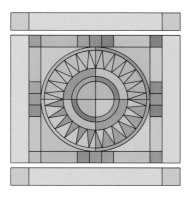

4. BORDERS 3 & 4: Cut Border 3 pieces - 2 pieces 28½" long and 2 pieces 30½" long. Stitch short pieces to sides. Press. Stitch long pieces to top and bottom. Repeat for Border 4 with 2 pieces 30½" and 31½".

5. BORDER 5: Cut 4 purple/turquoise strips 27½" long. Stitch corner squares to each end of 2 purple/turquoise pieces. Press. Stitch to sides of quilt. Press. Stitch 2 corner squares to each end of remaining pieces. Press. Stitch to top and bottom of quilt. Press.

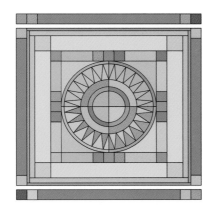

6. BORDER 6: Stitch appliques to blocks (except for suns), centered and at least ½" from raw edges. Stitch blocks into borders as shown. Press. Stitch side borders to quilt. Press. Repeat with top and bottom borders.

Make 8   Make 2   Make 8   Make 4

Border 6 Sides - Make 2

Border 6 Top & Bottom - Make 2

Lil' Duds

Continued from page 10

4. BORDER: Stitch short pieces to sides of quilt. Press. Stitch corner squares to each end of each long piece. Press. Stitch to top and bottom of quilt. Press.

5. LAYER & QUILT: Cut backing to same size as batting. Layer and quilt as desired. Trim backing and batting even with quilt top.

6. BIND: Stitch binding strips end to end. Press in half lengthwise, wrong sides together. Bind quilt using ⅜" seam allowance.

Continued on page 35

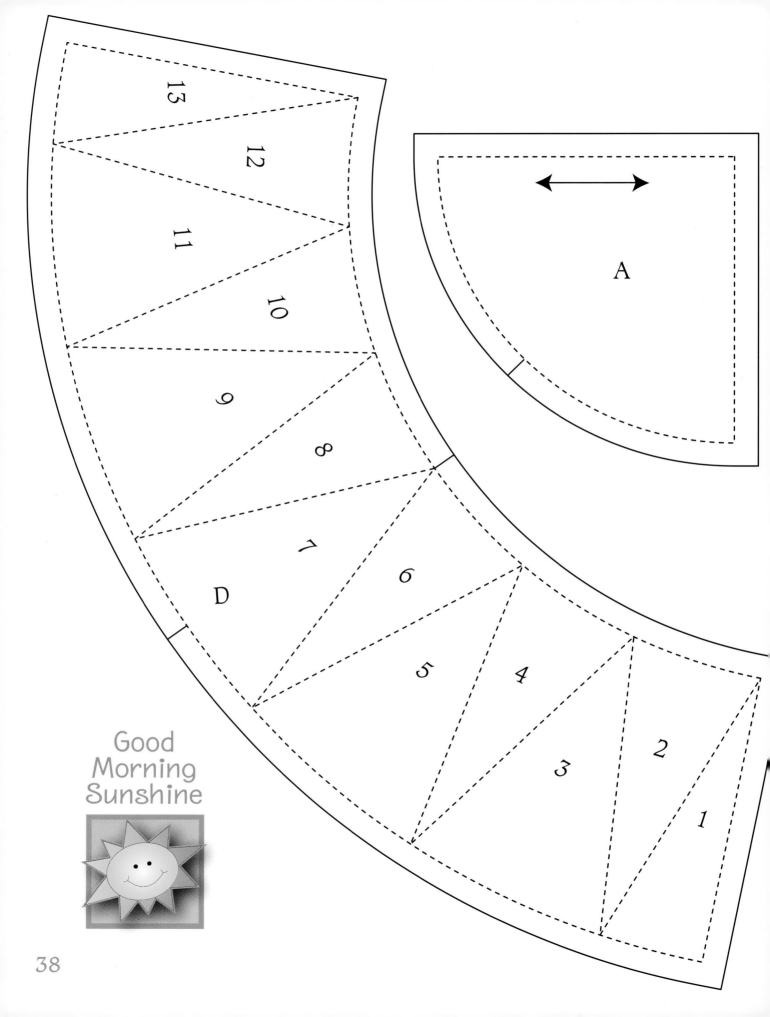

13

12

11

10

9

8

7

6

5

4

3

2

1

D

A

Good
Morning
Sunshine

38

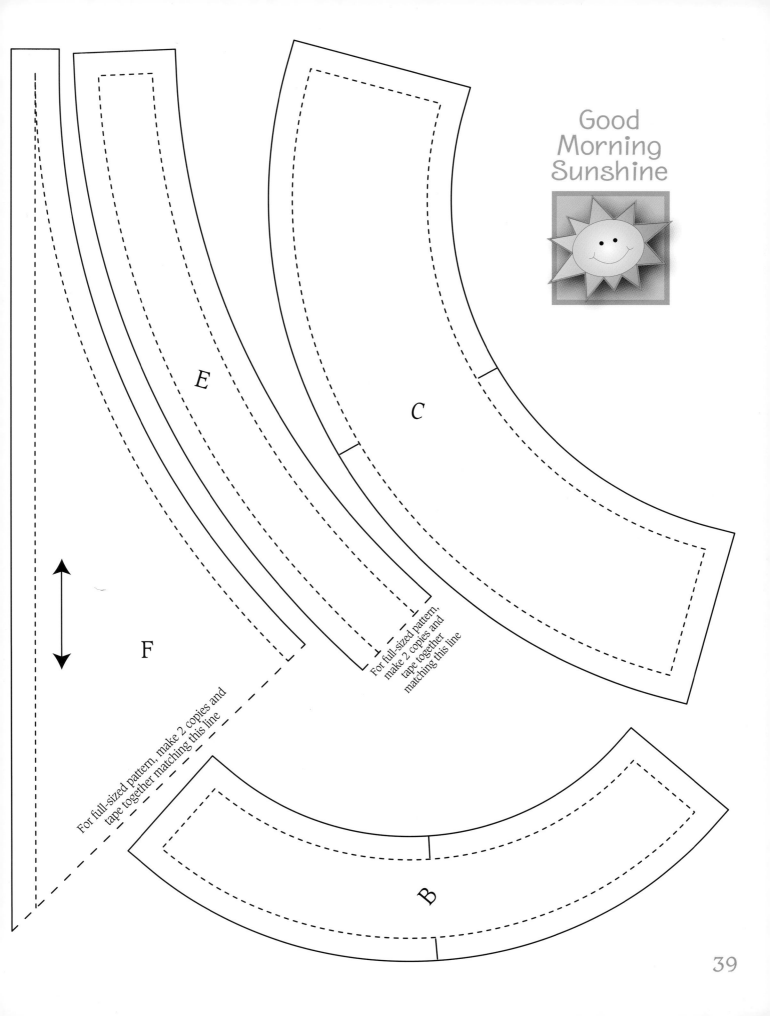

Good
Morning
Sunshine

E

C

F

For full-sized pattern, make 2 copies and tape together matching this line

For full-sized pattern, make 2 copies and tape together matching this line

B

39

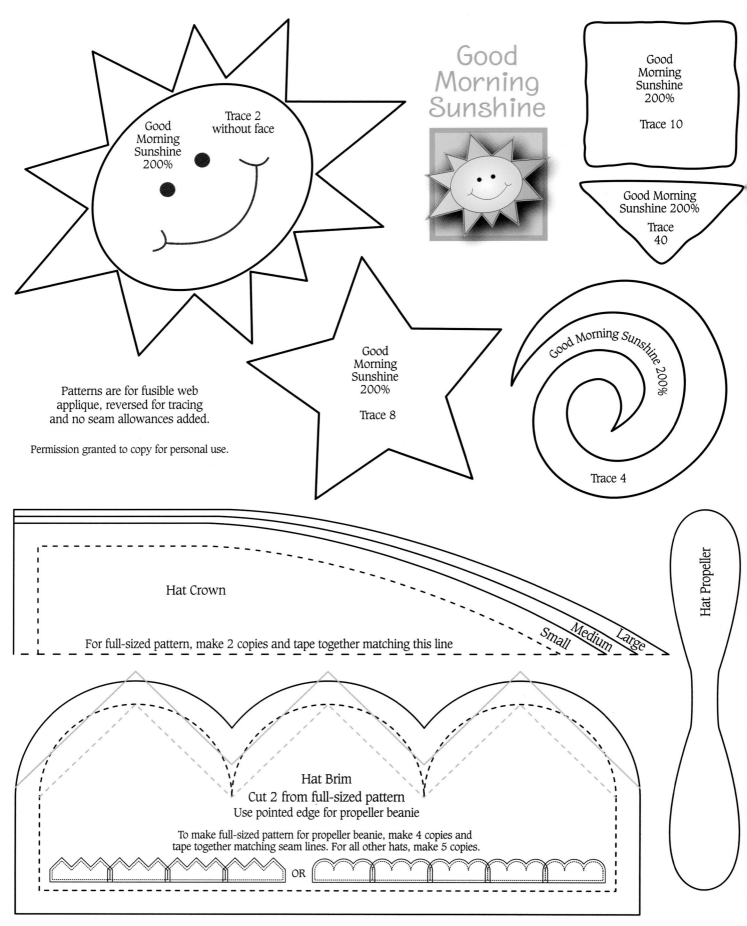

Good
Morning
Sunshine

Good Morning Sunshine 200%

Trace 2 without face

Good
Morning
Sunshine
200%

Good
Morning
Sunshine
200%

Trace 10

Good Morning
Sunshine 200%

Trace
40

Patterns are for fusible web
applique, reversed for tracing
and no seam allowances added.

Permission granted to copy for personal use.

Good
Morning
Sunshine
200%

Trace 8

Good Morning Sunshine 200%

Trace 4

Hat Crown

For full-sized pattern, make 2 copies and tape together matching this line

Small   Medium   Large

Hat Propeller

Hat Brim
Cut 2 from full-sized pattern
Use pointed edge for propeller beanie

To make full-sized pattern for propeller beanie, make 4 copies and
tape together matching seam lines. For all other hats, make 5 copies.

OR

40

Choo Choo

Use fine-point permanent marker for face

Trace 2
Trace 1 reversed

Trace 2
Trace 1 reversed

Patterns are for fusible web applique, reversed for tracing and no seam allowances added.

Permission granted to copy for personal use.

Trace 3

Trace 3

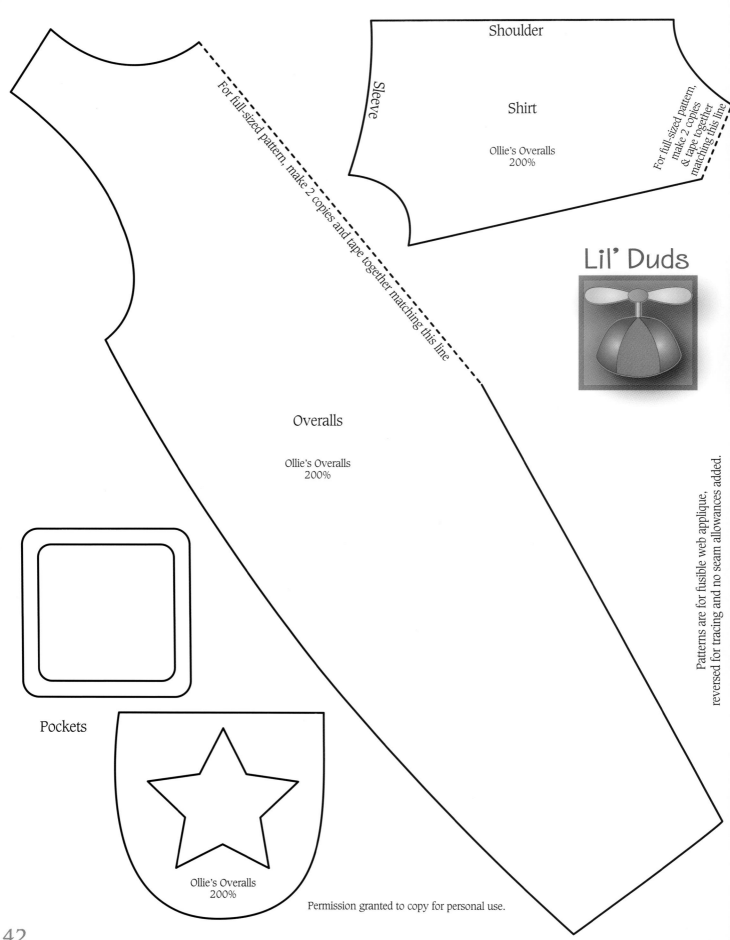

Shoulder

Sleeve

Shirt

Ollie's Overalls
200%

For full-sized pattern, make 2 copies and tape together matching this line

For full-sized pattern, make 2 copies & tape together matching this line

Lil' Duds

Overalls

Ollie's Overalls
200%

Patterns are for fusible web applique, reversed for tracing and no seam allowances added.

Pockets

Ollie's Overalls
200%

Permission granted to copy for personal use.

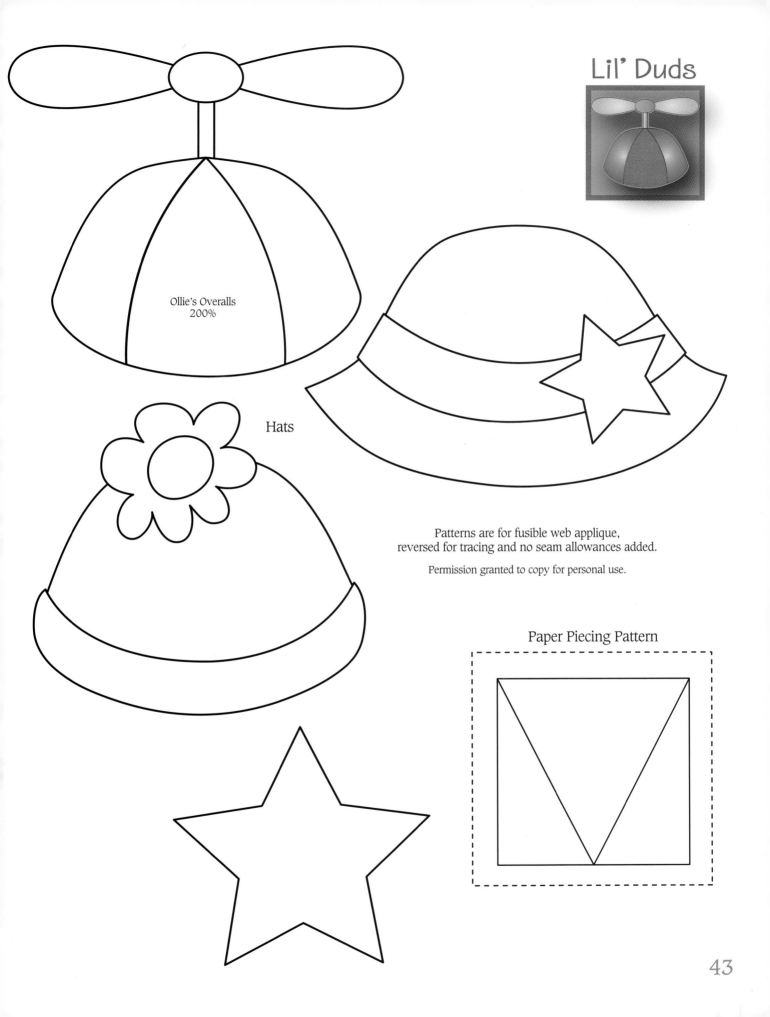

Lil' Duds

Ollie's Overalls
200%

Hats

Patterns are for fusible web applique,
reversed for tracing and no seam allowances added.

Permission granted to copy for personal use.

Paper Piecing Pattern

43

Sling - 200%

Enlarge or reduce on a copier to fit your project!
Permission granted to copy for personal use.

Use fine-point
permanent marker
for eyes

Stitching
Lines

Flanged Pillow - 200%

Penguin Parade
large penguin
200%

Embroider
antennae

Embroider
antennae

Blanket
200%

Patterns are for fusible web applique,
reversed for tracing and no seam allowances added.

Diaper Bag
200%

Embroider rope

Enlarge or reduce on a copier to fit your project!
Permission granted to copy for personal use.

Embroider antennae

Patterns are for fusible
web applique, reversed for tracing
and no seam allowances added.

45

Use fine-point permanent marker for faces

Flanged Pillow 200%

Patterns are for fusible web applique, reversed for tracing and no seam allowances added.

Enlarge or reduce on a copier to fit your project!
Permission granted to copy for personal use.

ABCDEFG

HIJKLMNOP

QRSTUVW

XYZ&!.,? 123

4567890

reversed for tracing and no seam allowances added.

Lily Rose - 200%
Blanket - 200%

Enlarge or reduce on a copier to fit your project!

 Resources

The following items may be ordered from us by mail, web, or phone.

Baby Bumper Pads by Fairfield	6 precut foam pieces with pattern for covers by Possibilities®	$17.95 + postage
Nurture Nest by Fairfield	U-shaped support pillow form with pattern for cover	$24.99 + postage
EQ Printables	6 cotton lawn inkjet fabric sheets 8½ x11″	$18.95 + postage
…and the Three Bears	Stuffed bear pattern with color cover & full directions for 3 sizes	$6.95 + postage
Teddy Bear Magic	Bear pattern with color cover & full directions (fiberfill + filler beads)	$6.95 + postage
Quackers	Stuffed duck pattern with color cover & full directions	$6.95 + postage
Gathered Dust Ruffle	Download from our website or receive by mail	$2.00 + postage
Ruffled Blanket	Download from our website or receive by mail	$2.00 + postage
Ruffled Pillow	Download from our website or receive by mail	$2.00 + postage

Possibilities® Great American Quilt Factory, Inc.
8970 East Hampden Avenue • Denver, Colorado 80231
1.800.474.2665 • www.greatamericanquilt.com • www. possibilitiesquilt.com

Quilt Label

Make a color transfer of the quilt label on fabric. EQ Printables, above in resources list, works great for this! Use a permanent marking pen to fill in the details. Cut out, leaving a seam allowance. Turn under seam allowance and hand stitch to back of baby quilt.

WELCOME BABY

Made especially for _____

Born on the _____ day of _____, _____

Crafted with love by _____

Name of Quilt: _____   Date Completed: _____